1. The principal reason why American medium tank battalions entered the North African campaign equipped with the M3 Lee instead of the more modern M4 Sherman was that President Franklin D. Roosevelt had generously insisted that all available supplies of the latter should be sent to the British Eighth Army, then fighting its series of climactic actions at El Alamein. The main disadvantage of the Lee was that its 75mm main armament was mounted in a sponson, thereby making it difficult for tank commanders to make full use of such natural cover as the terrain offered. This example, an M3A5 belonging to the 1st Armoured Division, has a counterweight fitted to the 75mm muzzle to assist the gyro-stabiliser, which operated in the vertical plane only. The vehicle was photographed on the Kasserine Pass sector in February 1943. (USAMHI)

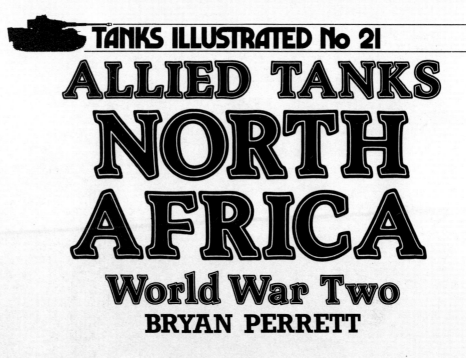

TANKS ILLUSTRATED No 21

ALLIED TANKS
NORTH
AFRICA
World War Two
BRYAN PERRETT

a&ap

ARMS AND ARMOUR PRESS

Introduction

Published in 1986 by Arms & Armour Press Ltd.,
2–6 Hampstead High Street, London NW3 1QQ.

Distributed in the United States by Sterling
Publishing Co. Inc., 2 Park Avenue, New York,
N.Y.10016.

British Library Cataloguing in Publication Data:
Perrett, Bryan
Allied tanks North Africa, World War Two.—
(Tanks illustrated; v. 21)
1. World War, 1939–1945—Campaigns—Africa,
North   2. World War, 1939–1945—Tank warfare
I. Title   II. Series
940.54'23   D766.82

ISBN 0-85368-775-7

Editing, design and artwork by Roger Chesneau.
Typesetting by Typesetters (Birmingham) Ltd.
Printed and bound in Italy
by GEA/GEP in association with
Keats European Ltd., London.

The period which began with the defeat of Rommel's army at El Alamein and ended with the final Axis surrender in Tunisia is of great interest for three important reasons. First, the British Eighth Army crowned its decisive victory with a difficult 2,000-mile advance across Africa. Second, when the Allied First Army landed in Algeria and Morocco the American contingent was making the US Army's first major contribution to the Second World War. The Americans were full of enthusiasm but so inexperienced that at first some units were barely able to look after themselves in the field, and inevitably they sustained reverses, of which the best remembered is that at Kasserine Pass. However, in a way that is uniquely American, the causes of those defeats were scrupulously examined and ruthlessly eliminated, so that the campaign in North Africa can be said to be the foundation stone upon which the combat techniques so successfully employed by the US Army for the remainder of the war were constructed. There were, too, actions in which American troops distinguished themselves brilliantly and, of course, the campaign proved to be a crucial turning point in the career of the then little-known Maj. Gen. George S. Patton Jr.

The third reason is that the six months which elapsed between November 1942 and May 1943 witnessed the employment of a wider variety of Allied armoured fighting vehicles than any other period of the war. There were Crusaders, Valentines and Churchills, Stuarts, Lees, Grants and Shermans, Renault R35s and even First World War FT 17s. There were armoured cars of various types, self-propelled guns, tank destroyers, armoured personnel carriers and assault engineer vehicles. For anyone with even a passing interest in the subject, the differing operational practices of the First and Eighth Armies make this a particularly fascinating and rewarding area of study.

Bryan Perrett

◀2
2. The 2nd New Zealand Divisional Cavalry Regiment was equipped with Stuarts and tracked carriers. After Alamein, the division was to have been withdrawn from the desert for service in the South Pacific against the Japanese, but at the request of Churchill and the Combined Chiefs of Staff, who prized its fighting qualities highly, it was permitted by the New Zealand Parliament to remain in the Mediterranean theatre of war, taking part in the advance across Africa and the fighting in Tunisia. (RAC Tank Museum)

▲3   ▼4

3. The victors of Alamein. The commanders of these M4A1s (known in British service as Sherman IIs) have the natural self-confidence of men who have won a decisive victory and crossed a continent. As part of Montgomery's deception plan prior to the battle, tanks were disguised as lorries, being concealed beneath dummy cabs and canopies which rested on rails welded to the hull sides. When the disguises were dropped the rails remained and provided an ingenious method of stowing personal kit. In some British units aerial sections were painted a sand colour or even white, thereby making them less conspicuous. (USAMHI)

4. Excluding units equipped with infantry tanks, most of the Eighth Army's armoured regiments at this period consisted of one light squadron with Crusaders or Stuarts and two heavy squadrons with Grants and/or Shermans; a further exception was provided by the 4th Light Armoured Brigade, which began Second Alamein with 67 Stuarts and 14 Grants. After the battle much priceless track mileage was saved by using tank transporters for the second echelon of the advance into Libya. (National Army Museum)

5. Breakout: an armoured regiment equipped with Crusaders and Shermans breaks away from the constraints imposed by the minefields of the El Alamein battlefield. (Imperial War Museum)

6. During its early stages the pursuit of the Afrika Korps was hampered by fuel shortages and torrential rain – the fact that greatcoats and heavier clothing are here being worn during the day gives some indication of the change in the weather. The location can be identified as Mersa Matruh, which was entered on 7 November by the 8th Armoured Brigade (3 RTR, Sherwood Rangers Yeomanry and Staffordshire Yeomanry). The 2nd Armoured Brigade (the Queen's Bays, 9th Lancers and 10th Hussars) was positioned some fifteen miles to the south awaiting replenishment, and the 22nd Armoured Brigade (1 RTR, 5 RTR and 4th County of London Yeomanry) was operating in the gap between the two. (Imperial War Museum)

6▼

▲7

7. During Second Alamein, direct support for infantry operations was provided by the 200 Valentines of the 23rd Armoured Brigade (8th, 40th, 46th and 50th Royal Tank Regiments). After the battle the brigade took part in the Eighth Army's advance to Tunisia, initially with 40 RTR only, joined by 50 RTR in time for the capture of Tripoli. 50 RTR were ferried on tank transporters for most of the way, but 40 RTR made the whole journey on their tracks and some of their Valentines had done over 3,000 miles when Tunisia was reached, a remarkable tribute to the quality of Vickers' engineering. (Author's Collection)

8. Despite the censor's attempt to eliminate the unit's tactical number, these Sherman M4A1s in line ahead have been identified as belonging to 'C' Squadron, the Queen's Bays, the senior regiment of the 2nd Armoured Brigade, 1st Armoured Division. The division's charging rhino emblem can be seen on the offside track-guards of the two leading vehicles. (RAC Tank Museum)

9. The lean lines of the Crusader III, armed with a 6pdr gun, provide an interesting contrast with the rounder form of the Sherman M4A1. (RAC Tank Museum)

▲8 ▼9

10. An unidentified M4A1 squadron marches past the saluting base with troops in line at a post-Alamein parade, guns swinging to the left and dipping in salute. (RAC Tank Museum)

11. The Matilda Scorpion was a normal gun tank fitted with a Ford or Bedford engine on the right of the hull. This drove a flail ahead of the vehicle, exploding mines in its path. Twelve Scorpions were used at Alamein, manned by crews from 42 and 44 RTR; they were employed at night, two rear-facing red lights being mounted on the antennae at the rear of the vehicle to indicate its position to following troops in the enveloping dust cloud. After the battle there was a great deal of tidying up to do but mines did not influence the conduct of operations again until Tunisia was reached. (Imperial War Museum)

12. The A15 Cruiser Tank Mk. VI Crusader first saw action during Operation 'Battleaxe' in June 1941 and was in service for the remainder of the war in North Africa; the Crusader Is and IIs had a 2pdr main armament, the Crusader III a 6pdr. The tank's early actions were plagued by breakdowns arising from clogged air filters, snapped fan belts and broken gear selectors, but in time these problems were sorted out and the vehicle became popular with its crews, who enjoyed the comfortable ride provided by the 'big wheel' Christie suspension. German anti-tank gunners found the Crusader's speed unsettling, but the fact remained that by 1942 the tank was under-gunned and under-armoured for the tasks it was required to perform. (Author's Collection)

10▲

11▲   12▼

▲13

13. A Grant squadron advancing in open order. The essential difference between the Lee and the Grant was evident in the 37mm turret. The Lee turret was too small to accommodate the tank radio, but British practice required the loader to operate the set in the turret, where close contact could be maintained with the vehicle commander. The Grant turret, therefore, was designed to remedy this deficiency, the effect of the modification being to reduce the size of the crew to six, one fewer than was required for the Lee. (RAC Tank Museum)

14. Stuarts in a mild dust storm; the only advantage of the latter is that it will make the flies disappear for a while! The tank on the left is flying what might be a navigator's flag and a tin-foil pennon, whilst that on the right is flying an ordinary cloth pennon which will soon be blown to tatters. The length of aerial that has been erected suggests that communications are extremely difficult. (Imperial War Museum)

15. A County of London Yeomanry squadron advancing with troops in line abreast on good hard going. The tanks are painted in the camouflage scheme used at Alamein and show so little sign of wear that they are obviously a recent issue. A blade-vane sight has been fitted to the turret just forward of the cupola, enabling the commander to verify the lay of the main armanent. (National Army Museum)

16. A B-25 Mitchell bomber makes a dramatically low pass to identify a Sherman squadron as being friendly. The waves and the relaxed attitudes of the tank crews demonstrate the complete air superiority enjoyed by the Eighth Army during its long advance. Notice how far back from the crest the tanks have to lie before they are turret-down. (National Army Museum)

▼14

15▲ 16▼

▲17

17. A squadron commander briefs his troop leaders aboard his hull-down Sherman. With more powerful tank guns coming into service, the range at which engagements were fought was beginning to open and the choice of position was becoming ever more important. At 1,000yds the turret presents a small and temporary target, since the tank commander will change position after firing two or perhaps three rounds. (National Army Museum)

18. Stand-to. A Crusader squadron remains on full alert while infantry dig in at last light. The tanks are all turret-down to the enemy with the exception of one of the pair in the exact centre of the picture, which has gone hull-down while its commander observes. After dusk the infantry commander will release the tanks when he is satisfied that their presence is no longer required. They will then retire into close leaguer some distance to the rear, replenish their

fuel and ammunition, and carry out essential maintenance. (National Army Museum)

19. Ease of maintenance was a virtue for which the Stuart was renowned: even in spartan conditions such as this it was a simple matter to remove the entire turret assembly, which rested on three rollers set 120 degrees apart. (Imperial War Museum)

20. A roadwheel is changed with assistance from the squadron fitters, whose mobile workshop truck is seen in the background. This type of damage usually arose as a result of shellfire or mines, but in this instance it has been possible to move the tank on to hard standing before starting work. Those men not involved are cleaning personal weapons; note that the rifle lying across the engine deck has its working parts protected from grit by being carefully wrapped in cloth. (Imperial War Museum)

▼18

▲21 ▼22

21. 'Cheetah', of 'C' Squadron, 40 RTR, was almost certainly the squadron navigator's tank – witness the sun compass seen on the extreme right of the photograph with a pale blue flag flying above. The lettering is red, shaded black, but in other respects the tank is painted in the familiar light stone and green colour scheme of the period. The illustration emphasizes how small the Valentine was, a fact which the enemy found disconcerting since it was able to take advantage of the gentlest fold in the ground for cover. (Imperial War Museum)

22. An officer of the 51st Highland Division enjoys an informal few minutes with a 23rd Armoured Brigade tank crew. The infantryman's rifle will make him less conspicuous among his men, but the trained sniper would also look for other tell-tale signs such as binoculars, map cases and hand signals directed at subordinates. Note the blade-vane line-up sight welded to the Valentine's turret roof, and the pennon cut from tin foil and painted. (Imperial War Museum)

23. A Valentine of 50 RTR being lifted forward by a Diamond-T of No. 1 Tank Transporter Company, Royal Army Service Corps, whose emblem, a giant holding a tank above his head, is seen on the door of the tractor unit. The transporter crews regarded themselves as the élite of their corps. (Australian War Memorial)

24. 40 RTR, with Gordon Highlanders aboard, enters Tripoli, 23 January 1943. Less than two years earlier these same Tripolitanians had welcomed Rommel and his troops to Africa with equal enthusiasm. (Imperial War Museum)

▲25

25. Tank commanders of 'B' Squadron, 40 RTR, enjoy a break during the advance to Tripoli. At this period the regiment was working with the 51st (Highland) Division, and because it was constantly brawling with Rommel's rearguards on the coastal sector it acquired the unofficial title 'Monty's Foxhounds', with Montgomery's full approval, so becoming the only unit ever to bear the future Field Marshal's name. The photograph contains two reminders of what soldiering in the desert was like: first, those who had no use for tobacco were wise to carry a fly-swat; and, second, unless the smallest cut was cleaned and bandaged promptly it could turn into a painful desert sore which might take weeks to heal. (Author's Collection)

26. Supply and reinforcement by sea was as important to the continuance of the Eighth Army's advance as that by land. After Tobruk had been recaptured, the town became the army's rail-head and principal 'export' harbour from which supplies and equipment were shipped successively to Benghazi, Buerat and Tripoli. These tanks seems to have come ashore from the LCTs in the background. (National Army Museum)

▼26

27. A Valentine of the 23rd Armoured Brigade passing through the village of Ben Gardane, 25 miles into Tunisia. To eyes accustomed only to the desert, the Tunisian landscape seemed unbelievably green and cultivated. The tank probably belongs to 40 RTR, for although the censor has eliminated the unit's tactical number the names of 50 RTR's tanks all began with the letter R whereas the Fortieth were allowed considerable latitude. The original name 'Helen' is just visible on the bow plate, with 'Marg' scrawled below, suggesting a change of heart by somebody. Note that the headlights have been turned inwards to eliminate reflection. (Imperial War Museum)

28. During the night of 20 March 1943 the 50th (Northumbrian) Division, with 50 RTR in support, crossed the Wadi Zigzaou and effected a penetration of the formidable Mareth Line. The 15th Panzer Division counterattacked at once, and throughout the next day 50 RTR's under-gunned Valentines held them off while the British infantry completed their withdrawal. The regiment lost 27 tanks and its commanding officer, Lt. Col. Cairns, was killed, but its gallant and resolute defence earned it four Military Crosses, six Military Medals and five Mentions in Despatches. The operation served to hold German attention on the coastal sector while the bulk of the Eighth Army carried out a wide sweep south of the Matmata Hills, outflanking the Mareth Line at a stroke. The photograph shows one of the 50th's Valentines knocked out on the enemy bank of the Wadi Zigzaou. (Author's Collection)

▲29

29. Another view of 50 RTR's gallant action at Mareth. The Valentine has been literally ripped apart by an internal explosion: blast produces strange effects, and in this case it has simply turned the turret over on to its roof. (Author's Collection)

30. 'Respond', of the 50th Royal Tank Regiment, with a full complement of the 51st Division's battle-hardened 'Jocks' aboard. 50 RTR was the third armoured regiment of the 23rd Armoured

Brigade; the other regiments were 40 RTR and 46 RTR, both of which were originally raised in Liverpool, hence the choice of the mythical liver bird as the brigade's emblem. A fourth regiment, the veteran 8 RTR, joined the brigade for Second Alamein, and together the four regiments mustered 194 Valentines and fought in support of the 1st South African, 2nd New Zealand, 9th Australian and 51st (Highland) Divisions. (Imperial War Museum)

▼30

31. The Bishop self-propelled gun consisted of a Valentine hull and chassis with the turret replaced by a box of thin armour mounting a 25pdr gun-howitzer. It was slow across country and cramped to work in, and because it carried only 32 rounds of ammunition it was often seen towing a conventional limber. The Bishop was issued to 121 Field Regiment RA, which fired in support of the all-Valentine 23rd Armoured Brigade at Alamein and beyond. It remained in service until the Sicilian campaign. An attempt has been made to reinforce the driving compartment of this example with sandbags. (Imperial War Museum)

32. A rear view of the Bishop, showing the battery letter on the superstructure and troop markings on the skirting plate. The crew's water supply is contained in the notorious 'flimsies' which would burst at the seams at the first hint of rough handling. The vehicle has been fitted with an auxiliary fuel jettison tank. Compare with the previous photograph. (Imperial War Museum)

32▼

▲34

33. (Previous spread) The battle of the Wadi Akarit took place on 5 April 1943, with 40 and 50 RTR supporting respectively the 50th and 51st Infantry Divisions. The lessons of Mareth had been learned, and many of the tanks towed the infantry's 6pdr anti-tank guns across the anti-tank ditch so that when the enemy's counterattack came in it was easily defeated. After Wadi Akarit the emphasis of the fighting in Tunisia shifted to the First Army's front in the mountains. The photograph shows a pilot's-eye view of a 40 RTR squadron rally-point after the battle, including fuel and ammunition lorries and the fitters' vehicles; to the left, a column of Italian prisoners is being marched off. (Imperial War Museum)

34. The partly flooded anti-tank ditch at the Wadi Akarit, showing the causeways constructed across the obstacle. The Sherman about to cross almost certainly belongs to the 4th County of London Yeomanry, which had been transferred temporarily from the 22nd to the 23rd Armoured Brigade for this operation; one of the latter's Valentines can be seen on the right of the photograph. (Imperial War Museum)

35. One of the 4th CLY's Shermans crossing the Wadi Akarit anti-tank ditch on the Highland Division's sector. The sappers have thrown down the sides of the ditch to form a causeway. (Imperial War Museum)

▼35

36▲

36. After storming the Wadi Akarit Line, the Eighth Army effected a junction with the US II Corps at Gafsa. Here some of the first British troops to arrive exchange greetings with the crew of an American M3 Stuart moving north as part of the general redeployment. It is interesting to note that by now the Americans, like the British, have dispensed with the M3's sponson machine guns and put the space thus gained to better use. (USAMHI)

37. This Sherman crew have managed to persuade some local infantrymen to help them lay out their track in the cool of the early morning. The Germans often mined the wadi crossing points and it seems probable that this was the cause of the damage. The work involved in repairing and replacing the track is heavy – especially so on soft ground – and the smiles have obviously been provoked by some remark of the visiting US Army Signal Corps photographer. The tank still shows weathered traces of the charcoal grey and sand colour scheme in which it fought at Alamein. The location is not specified, but the combination of landscape and vegetation suggests that the photograph was taken in southern Tunisia in April 1943. (USAMHI)

37▼

▲38 ▼39

38. An AEC Mk. I armoured car troop of the Royal Dragoons seen during the closing days of the campaign near Enfidaville. The AEC was an ingenious design which incorporated many components of the Matador gun tractor, and the Mk. I employed the same turret as the 2pdr marks of Valentine. The car weighed 11 tons and had a maximum speed of 36mph. The Royals were among the first troops to break out into open desert at Alamein but the nature of the fighting in Tunisia offered less scope for armoured car operations once the lines had stabilized in the hills. In more recent years The Royals have amalgamated with the Royal Horse Guards (The Blues) to form the Blues and Royals, a half-squadron of which saw action during the Falklands War. (Maj. K. G. Balfour)

39. Operation 'Torch', the Allied landings in North Africa, witnessed the arrival of numerous types of vehicle which had not seen action previously. This American M2 halftrack being swung over the side of a British transport into a waiting LCM off Oran has actually been converted to the tank destroyer role by the addition of a gunshield and the 37mm gun stripped from the unpopular Dodge ¾-ton M6 Gun Motor Carriage, although the weapon itself is completely hidden by stowed equipment. The conversion, of which there were several minor variations, was known as the M2 37mm GMC, and this example belonged to the 601st Tank Destroyer Battalion. A further point of interest is that the white recognition stars have been painted on to a medium blue roundel in accordance with instructions issued to all US troops entering the Mediterranean theatre of war. The majority of units ignored the directive and the custom was quickly abandoned. The vehicle is painted overall in standard US Army olive drab, with a white line across the bottom of the rear hull to assist night driving in convoy. (USAMHI)

40. Here, the M2 has been stowed aboard the LCM and a towed 37mm anti-tank gun is being hoisted into the remaining space. This weapon was comparable in performance to the British 2pdr and was therefore obsolete, but it remained in service with the Tank Destroyer Force until replaced by the towed 3inch anti-tank gun M1. (USAMHI)

43▲

41. The British beach-master's party braces the LCM against a sudden yaw as an M2 halftrack armoured personnel carrier leaves the vessel. In places the Vichy French forces offered a token resistance but in general the landings seemed more like large-scale exercises than actual war; the beach-master's canvas shoes add to the slightly unreal holiday atmosphere. (USAMHI)

42. Part of the US 2nd Armored Division passing through a town in French Morocco just after the Allied landings. The attitude of the French officer is eloquent of wounded national pride; his native troops are less hurt, but understandably confused. (USAMHI)

43. The Scout Car M3A1 possessed four-wheel drive and was usually armed with a single machine gun on a skid-rail mounting. Over 20,000 were built by the White Motor Company during the Second World War and, indeed, the vehicle is more generally referred to as the White Scout Car; a few can still be found serving in the armies of smaller nations. This example belongs to a reconnaissance unit and is seen leaving Oran on D-Day, but the vehicle was capable of a wide variety of uses such as command car, mortar carrier, light armoured personnel carrier and artillery observation vehicle. (USAMHI)

44. A 105mm Howitzer Motor Carriage M7 belonging to one of the 1st Armored Division's armoured artillery battalions reverses ashore from its LCT at Oran, 9 November 1942. In British service the M7 was known as the Priest, probably because of the commander's 'pulpit' located at the forward right-hand corner of the vehicle; subsequently, most British self-propelled artillery equipments were named after church officials (Bishop, Sexton, Deacon, etc.), a tradition maintained to this day. (USAMHI)

44▼

▲45

45. An M3 Stuart light tank company, probably Company 'C' of the 1/1st Armored Regiment, preparing to move out during the early days of the campaign. One unfortunate feature of the Stuart's design was the limited internal fuel capacity of 56 gallons. This seriously restricted the vehicle's operational radius and the British, in whose hands the Stuart first saw action during Operation 'Crusader' (November 1941), employed two additional 25-gallon jettison tanks to remedy the defect. The US Army decided to do likewise and details of the cylindrical jettison tanks can be seen on the nearest vehicles. It is also interesting to note that at this period the sponson machine guns were still being fitted, although their negligible value was quickly evident. (USAMHI)

46. A recently landed M5 Stuart light tank of the US 1st Armored

Division passes a 7th Infantry rifle squad near Oran during the evening of D-Day. At this period 1st Armored, later known as 'Old Ironsides', contained two armoured regiments, the 1st and 13th, each consisting of one light Stuart battalion and two medium battalions. There were insufficient LCTs to disembark the medium battalions in adequate numbers, so the two light battalions landed first and were beefed up with a detachment of 75mm M3 tank destroyers. For the remainder of November 1943 the 1/1st and 1/13th Battalions were employed aggressively ahead of the main body of the First Army during its advance from Algeria into Tunisia, the former particularly so. For the landing itself, many vehicles in the leading wave were painted with the Stars and Stripes for political reasons. (USAMHI)

▼ 46

47 ▲

47. The 75mm Gun Motor Carriage M3 was the US Army's first standard tank destroyer and consisted of a marriage between the M3 halftrack and the M1897-A4 75mm gun, which was an American version of the famous French 'Soixante-Quinze'. The mounting was designed by an Ordnance officer, the then Maj. Robert J. Icks, who later achieved an international reputation for his writings on AFVs as well as for the generosity with which he shared his vast store of knowledge. The 'Seventy-Five' was a weapon which had to be treated with respect by its crews since it possessed a recoil of 43in and could knock a loader flat unless he was nippy about his business! The GMC M3 was adopted as the symbol of the Tank Destroyer Force and was depicted in orange-gold (the TDF's branch-of-service colour) on all company guidons. This example is shown at a workshop in North Africa and has clearly seen hard usage – witness the paint that has burned off the barrel. On the far right of the photograph is an early example of the 105mm HMC M7. (US Army)

48. The US 2nd Armored Division, subsequently nicknamed 'Hell on Wheels', landed in Morocco but was not as heavily engaged in the campaign as the 1st, to which it was similarly organized, its two armoured regiments being the 66th and 67th. This column of Stuarts is passing through Casablanca, the location confirmed by the sign outside the local branch of the French ex-servicemen's association, Legion Française des Combattants. (USAMHI)

48 ▼

▲49　▼50

49. Although minor engagements did take place between Vichy French and American armoured units immediately following the landings, these First World War Renault FTs, armed with a short 37mm gun, were wisely abandoned by their crews at Safi, Morocco, before misunderstandings could arise. Such sights must have provoked a sense of *déjà vu* in one senior American officer, Major General George S. Patton, who, as a young lieutenant-colonel had, on 12 September 1918, led the US Army's first tank attack with the two Renault FT battalions which formed his 304th Tank Brigade. (USAMHI)

50. The French also used Renault R35 infantry tanks to oppose the Allied landings. On 9 November 1942 a force of R35s approaching St. Lucien from the direction of Sidi-bel-Abbes was engaged and defeated by the Stuarts of the American 1/1st Armored Regiment. The two-man R35 was armed with a short 37mm gun and a 7.5mm co-axial machine gun. Some 1,600 had been built since 1935, but their design was hopelessly obsolete and they were not taken into Allied service. This example was photographed at a depot in Algeria, the crew having apparently expressed their willingness to join the Allies by means of a white flag. (RAC Tank Museum)

51. In November an Allied attempt to seize Tunis and Bizerta by *coup de main* failed narrowly because of the speed with which Axis reinforcements were shipped to Africa. The southern flank of the Allied thrust was made by a British battlegroup known as 'Blade Force', to which the American 1st/1st Tank Battalion was attached. The photograph shows one of the battalion's Stuarts returning from a forward patrol, passing through dug-in British infantry at the limit of 'Blade Force's advance. (Imperial War Museum)

52. These Daimler armoured cars of 5 Troop, 'C' Squadron, 1st Derbyshire Yeomanry, the armoured car regiment of the 6th Armoured Division, show the red-white-red oblong employed by the First Army; the division's mailed fist emblem is just visible on the nearside mudguard. The regiment had a cavalryman's field day when its cars, accompanied by the Stuart light tanks of the US 1st/1st Tank Battalion, stormed across Djedeida airfield on 26 November, catching 37 Ju 87 dive-bombers in the act of re-arming. (Imperial War Museum)

53. The narrow failure of 'Blade Force' left British and American equipment in German hands, and some, such as this Valentine seen in German markings on the Tunis waterfront, was taken into service and used against its former owners. Compare with the Valentine used as a decoy at Thala, photograph 76. (Author)

51▲

52▲   53▼

▲54

54. A careful study of the early campaigns of the war had convinced the US Army of the importance of organic anti-aircraft defence, and each tank destroyer battalion contained eighteen twin AA .50cal machine guns mounted on M2 or M3 halftracks. In this case the vehicle has only just come ashore and is towing a 37mm anti-tank gun across the beach. The 'One Dozen Roses' are presumably the crew; it would be interesting to learn whether their Master Sergeant saw them in this light! (USAMHI)

55. The sheer scale of the US Army's expansion brought with it its own problems, and in some cases only experience could translate unproven theory into practice. This applied even in such simple matters as a tank crew learning to live together in the field, and anyone who has ever served aboard an armoured vehicle will view

this scene with horror, if not total disbelief. Instead of only taking off the vehicle what is actually needed – and promptly replacing it – this crew of new arrivals are living like gypsies. Visible amidst the clutter is somebody's bed; ration packs; personal clothing and steel helmets galore; tools large and small; and a partly stripped-down Browning machine gun. The soldier in the centre has just discovered the old military truth that operations are never planned to take place in the centre of any one map, but at the point where the corners of four or more sheets meet. The effect of an order to move can well be imagined, but the crew will learn very quickly from their mistakes. The marking on the tank's sponson shows that it belongs to the 2nd Platoon, Company 'E', 2nd Battalion, 13th Armored Regiment. (USAMHI)

▼55

56 ▲

56. This photograph of the same unit was taken only three days later and shows a remarkable transformation, although there is still room for considerable improvement. Two-man pup tents are not a good idea for tank crews, the use of the tank sheet as a lean-to bivouac being infinitely preferable, since it can accommodate everyone. Moreover, a standard order for sleeping can be established by a unit, with those most likely to be needed at short notice during the night, for example tank commanders and drivers, laying their bedrolls at the outer ends. (USAMHI)

57. By the beginning of December the lessons learned by the medium companies of the 13th Armored Regiment were clearly beginning to show. 'Kentucky', belonging to the 3rd Platoon, Company 'F', 2nd Battalion, can move at a moment's notice; even the camouflage net has been neatly rolled ready for lifting aboard, and the towing hawser has been carefully arranged so as not to foul the sponson door. (USAMHI)

57 ▼

▲58

58,59. These lessons applied to everyone, and not just to tank crews, as the company headquarters personnel of Company 'D', 2nd Battalion, 13th Armored Regiment demonstrate. (USAMHI)

60. Just the sort of photograph soldiers have been sending home since the Crimean War. In most respects this 2/13th crew give the impression of being grizzled veterans; on the other hand, stockinged feet are tempting providence in the land of the scorpion, confirming that they are very new to the desert. Of particular interest to AFV modellers is the fact that although every man is wearing the 'uniform' appropriate to the task he is currently performing, no two are dressed exactly alike – a quite normal situation in harbour areas. (USAMHI)

61. A Stuart, a Lee and an M3 halftrack photographed in Tunisia in December 1942. All three vehicles have been given a liberal coating of local mud to conform with their background. The Lee's markings indicate that the vehicle belongs to the 1st Armored Regiment's 3rd Battalion, Company 'I'. (RAC Tank Museum)

▼59

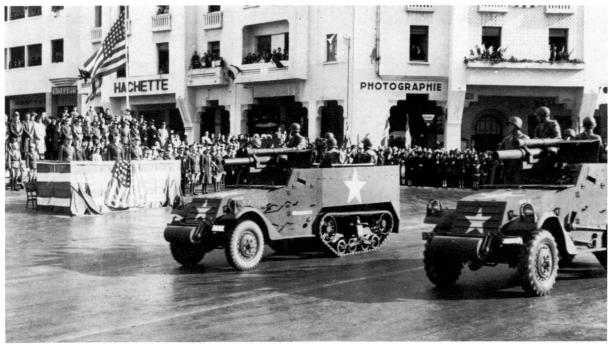

▲ 62

62. T19 105mm Howitzer Motor Carriages of the 2nd Armored Division drive past Gens. Patton and Nogues during a parade held in Rabat, Morocco. The letters 'USA' and the vehicle serial numbers have been painted in pale blue on the engine side armour, but other visible markings are in white. The vehicle nearest to the saluting base seems to be called 'Ironsides'. (USAMHI)

63. Another view of the same parade showing that the Stars and Stripes has been painted on the vehicles' right hull armour, just behind the commander's door. The T19 was a stop-gap weapon system which saw little service beyond the North African campaign, and it was replaced by the fully-tracked M7 105mm HMC. (USAMHI)

▼ 63

64 ▲

64. Initially the French possessed virtually no AFVs with which they could meet the Axis on equal terms, but as the Americans progressively replaced their M3 tank destroyers with M10s the former were handed over to them. In this case the new owners appear to have smeared the original paintwork with local mud which has then been allowed to dry. (Col. Robert J. Icks)

65. A French mechanized infantry unit, re-equipped with M3A1 scout cars, on parade during Bastille Day celebrations. The machine gun was mounted on a skid which ran right round the vehicle's interior. (USAMHI)

65 ▼

66. Once the French Army in North Africa decided to throw in its lot with the Allies it was rapidly re-equipped by the United States under the terms of the Lend-Lease Agreement. The *tricolore* painted on the side of this M4 being swung ashore at Casablanca in April 1943 indicates that it is destined for French use. The wooden crutch was fitted to keep the gun rigid during shipment, thereby reducing the possibility of damage to the gun control equipment. (USAMHI)

68. The first major encounter between American and German troops took place at Sidi Bou Zid on 14 February when two panzer divisions, the 10th and the 21st, attacked under cover of a sandstorm and cut off part of the 1st Armored Division's Combat Command 'A', a Sherman battalion being all but wiped out during an abortive relief attempt. The Americans were forced to withdraw and much equipment had to be abandoned in the process. In this photograph a Sherman tows a broken-down halftrack. (USAMHI)

67. The long lines of Shermans and Stuarts awaiting delivery to the French Army at an ordnance depot near Casablanca provide eloquent proof of the American genius for industrial flexibility and mass production. The United States has been at war for little more than a year, yet already she is equipping her own armies on an unprecedented scale and has become the arsenal of her allies. (USAMHI)

▲69 ▼70

69. French officers familiarize themselves with the M2 scout car, the jeep and other items of American equipment during a class held for this specific purpose at Algiers on 9 February 1943. It seems that the American 37mm anti-tank gun is also on the agenda but is being monopolized by a younger group! (USAMHI)

70. A group of officers watches a Sherman Mine Exploder T3E1 flail its way through a barbed wire entanglement. The T3 was an American version of the Matilda-based Scorpion, a number of which were used at Alamein, and this was one of an experimental series intended to employ the M4 in this role. None of these was successful, although the British Army did produce an excellent Sherman flail known as the Crab, designated Mine Exploder T4 in American service. (USAMHI)

71. A rare view of the Grant Scorpion III mine-clearing flail tank, a few of which were built in Tunisia in January 1943. The flail was driven by a 30hp Bedford engine located in a housing at the right-rear of the hull, supplemented by a second engine of the same type mounted at the left-rear on an improved version, the Grant Scorpion IV. In both versions the 75mm main armament had to be stripped out of its sponson mounting to provide clearance for the chains. (National Army Museum)

▼72　▲73

72. After their success at Sidi Bou Zid the Germans stormed their way through the Kasserine Pass and seemed set to inflict a crushing defeat on the Allied First Army. After the first shock of battle, however, the inexperienced Americans quickly learned to roll with the punch and in the last week of February hard fighting by the 1st Armored Division, the British 26th Armoured Brigade and the 1st Guards Brigade stabilized the situation and forced the Afrika Korps to retreat whence it had come. The photograph shows Capt. G. W. Meade of the 13th Armored Regiment examining the open terrain west of the Pass from the turret of his M4A1 Sherman. (USAMHI)

73. M3 Lees of the 2nd Platoon, Company 'I', 3rd Battalion, 13th Armored Regiment, approaching the front during the Kasserine Pass operations. At this period the 13th Armored's company markings consisted of a series of oblongs and squares placed at

different angles and in differing positions to each other. Thus, in 1st/13th, the oblongs were horizontal; in 2nd/13th they were vertical; and in 3rd/13th they leaned to the right, as shown. The 1st Armored operated a similar system of markings with oblongs and circles. In both cases the platoon number followed the company marking, but this is seldom seen. (US Army)

74. Some of the Calgary Regiment's Churchills landed at Dieppe and a six-strong trials unit was present during Second Alamein, but the first British regiment to take these tanks into action was 142 (Suffolk) Regiment RAC, which, together with the 1st Guards Brigade, was rushed south to Le Kef to counter the enemy's breakthrough in the Kasserine Pass area. Some of the regiment's tanks are here seen preparing for their first action on the Sbeitla-Sbiba road. (The Suffolk Regiment)

▲75　▼76

75. Valentines of the 26th Armoured Brigade (6th Armoured Division) moving through Thala to close the gap blown in the Allied line by Rommel's breakthrough at Kasserine Pass. The brigade consisted of the 16th/5th Queen's Royal Lancers, the 17th/21st Lancers and the 2nd Lothians and Border Horse. At this period its regiments were equipped with Valentines and Crusaders, squadrons consisting of three 2pdr Valentine troops, one 6pdr Crusader troop, and an SHQ troop of two Valentines and two 3inch howitzer close-support Crusaders. The object was to make the most of the available firepower resources but the mixture of infantry and cruiser tanks was not compatible and few regarded the arrangement as satisfactory. (Imperial War Museum)

76. This captured Valentine displays the runes of the 10th Panzer Division to the right of the driver's vision block, while the buffalo emblem of the 7th Panzer Regiment has been stencilled on the rear of the turret. This vehicle may have been the 'Trojan Horse' which led the attack on the 17th/21st Lancers' leaguer at Thala, with the turret crew sitting smoking on the outside. (Imperial War Museum)

77. The scene at Thala where an enemy tank column tried to break into the 17th/21st Lancer's leaguer area; after losing seven tanks in a fierce close-quarter night action, the Germans withdrew. This incident marked the high-water point of Rommel's advance. Shortly afterwards, the 26th Armoured Brigade exchanged its Valentines and Crusaders for Shermans. (Imperial War Museum)

78. The contrast between the diminutive Valentine and the mighty Tiger is such as to induce an awed silence rather than superfluous comment! (Imperial War Museum)

77▲ 78▼

▲79

79. The cavalier attitude displayed by Maj. Gen. Lloyd Fredendall, the commander of the US II Corps, directly contributed to the débâcle at Kasserine Pass and cost him his job. He was replaced by Maj. Gen. George S. Patton, seen here in his command car personally directing II Corps' attack from Gafsa towards Gabes on 15 March 1943. Unlike his predecessor, who had exercised a dubious command from a purpose-built headquarters many miles behind the lines, Patton firmly believed in forward control during a mobile battle; he was a notoriously hard taskmaster, but his unit commanders knew exactly where they stood with him. His M2 has been modified *in situ* by the provision of a bullet- and splinter-proof

gunshield forward and a similarly constructed cover aft extending over the map table and radio equipment, the whole producing a startling contrast with the facilities available in a modern armoured command vehicle. The general's blue and white metal pennant can be seen just forward of the gunshield. (USAMHI)

80. General Patton's command group speeds past the wreckage of several German tanks destroyed by Allied air activity near Mateur, April 1943. The Pz Kpfw IV has little interest for the general, since nearby lie the shattered remains of a Tiger, the track of which can be seen in the foreground. (USAMHI)

▼80

81. Another command group M2 drives past the wreck of the Tiger, the length of which has been foreshortened by the angle at which the picture is being taken. The immense force of the internal explosion has blown out an entire hull side and a complete track assembly, exposing the surviving torsion bars, several of which have sheared or been warped. The Tigers in Tunisia belonged to the 501st Heavy Tank Battalion and to the 1st Company of the 504th Heavy Tank Battalion and were the first to be encountered by the Western Allies. (USAMHI)

82. A smashed 'Eighty-Eight', one of two knocked out at point-blank range by Capt. E. D. Hollands of 'A' Squadron 51 RTR during an astonishing action at Steamroller Farm on 28 February 1943. This utterly wrecked the southern thrust of an important German counteroffensive codenamed '*Ochsenkopf*' (Bull's Head). (Imperial War Museum)

82▼

▲83 ▼84

83. After destroying the two 'Eighty-Eights', Hollands broke through into the enemy's rear, where he caught the German transport echelon and set it ablaze. Shortly afterwards he was joined by Lt. J. G. Kenton, and when the two Pz Kpfw IIIs shown here attempted to intervene in the battle they were promptly despatched. Altogether, the destruction wreaked by 'A' Squadron amounted to two Pz Kpfw IIIs, 25 wheeled vehicles, eight anti-tank guns of various types, two 20mm anti-aircraft guns and two 3in mortars, to which must be added some 200 personnel casualties. The British crews were greatly amused by the hysterical tone of an intercepted German transmission which described them as a 'mad tank battalion' whose Churchills had scaled 'impossible heights'. (Imperial War Museum)

84. Crews of the 1st Armored Regiment, 1st Armored Division, drawing M4 Shermans near Oran. This busy scene shows two crewmen in the centre scrubbing out the barrel of the nearest tank while the kneeling soldier checks through the vehicle tool kit prior

to stowing it. Closest to the camera, the tank commander ponders the full extent of what he has just signed for! (US Army)

85. A good frontal study of the 3in Gun Motor Carriage M10, taken towards the end of the fighting in Tunisia. The M10 remedied the principal defect in the M3 tank destroyer, namely lack of all-round traverse. The vehicle also possessed the advantage of using the same basic chassis and running gear as the M3/M4 medium tank series although, as can clearly be seen, the hull sides were sharply angled. (USAMHI)

86. An Allied convoy, escorted by an M3 Stuart, near El Guettar, 8 April 1943. The turret markings clearly indicate that the vehicle belongs to Company 'D', 2nd Battalion, 1st Armored Regiment. The air recognition star on the roof and the excellent convoy discipline are a reminder that the Allies did not possess complete air superiority. The leading truck is a British Bedford 3-ton. (USAMHI)

87. A company orders group of the 601st Tank Destroyer Battalion, held at El Guettar on 23 March 1943 only hours before the 10th Panzer Division launched a furious attack on the position. The 601st lost 21 of its 31 tank destroyers but knocked out 38 enemy tanks when the latter's progress was blocked by a minefield. Such encounters fully restored the Americans' confidence, shaken the previous month at Kasserine Pass. El Guettar was a classic tank destroyer battle, but there were other occasions over which Patton was sharply criticized by the TDF for the reckless use of its battalions, resulting in needless casualties. The vehicle nearest the camera is a command version of the M2 halftrack; in the background a 75mm GMC M3 has taken up a good hull-down position offering a wide field of fire across the plain below. (USAMHI)

88. An M5 Stuart of Company 'A', 899th Tank Destroyer Battalion, leading company headquarters vehicles along a road near Maknassy, 8 April 1943. In conditions such as these dust penetrated everything and goggles were an absolute necessity. Personal kit stowed in this manner had a short active service life expectancy. (USAMHI)

89. The battle of Pichen-Fondouk was an attempt to break into the rear of the 1st Italian Army as it withdrew from the Wadi Akarit. On the left 128 (Hampshire) Brigade and 51 RTR were to capture Pichon and the high ground north of the Fondouk Pass, whilst on the right the US 34th Infantry Division and 751 Tank Battalion were to take the high ground to the south; the 6th Armoured Division, led by the 26th Armoured Brigade, would then break through the pass and capture Kairouan, trapping the Italians. Here Churchills of 'C' Squadron 51 RTR move into position prior to the battle. (Imperial War Museum)

▲88   ▼89

90. 128 Brigade's attack was a limited success which was not exploited properly by the higher command, but the US 34th Infantry Division's attack was a complete failure. Consequently, 26th Armoured Brigade's leading regiment, the 17th/21st Lancers, suffered serious losses when trying to force the pass and they were compelled to abandon the attempt; a second attempt was made by the 16th/5th Lancers along the dry bed of the River Marguellil and this succeeded. Coming so soon after the débâcle at Kasserine, the battle of Pichon-Fondouk strained Anglo-American relations to the limit. The picture shows one of the 16th/5th's tanks moving off along the river bed, closed down and with only the commander's helmeted head showing. The First Army's Shermans lacked the side rails and sand shields fitted to those of the Eighth. (Imperial War Museum)

91. This Russian-built 76mm anti-tank gun adapted for German use has been eliminated by a near-miss with a high-explosive round. Well camouflaged and dug in so that their barrels just cleared the ground, such weapons invariably had the advantage over tanks until the latter were issued with their own HE ammunition. After that, once a gun position had been detected its life expectancy was short. (Imperial War Museum)

90▲   91▼

55

92. The M2 and M3 halftracks were very similar in appearance, but the latter was a little longer and possessed a rear access door. A canvas roof could be erected over the hull (the supports can be seen attached to the vehicle's side), but this was generally thought to be more trouble than it was worth. The crew have been given the task of removing empty ammunition containers, which could build up very quickly inside an artillery battery's lines, particularly if heavy programmes are being fired in static conditions. If it is wondered why an armoured vehicle is required to perform this chore, the answer is probably that the M3 has recently arrived with a consignment of live rounds, a dump of which can be seen on the left, and that it makes good sense for it to make the return run with a payload. (USAMHI)

▲93

93. In Tunisia the Churchill demonstrated its legendary ability to climb hills for the first time, confounding German officers who genuinely believed that their hill-top positions were tank-proof. The photograph shows two tanks of the North Irish Horse on the slopes of the notorious Longstop Hill, captured jointly with the 5th Buffs on 26 April. The tank on the left is a Mk. III (6pdr) and that on the right a Mk. I (2pdr in the turret and 3in howitzer in the front plate). Both vehicles have a rolled canvas apron tied to their front plate. This could be slung between the front horns, so blocking the blast of dust generated beneath the stationary tank's belly by the sirocco fan and preventing it from being drawn in through the forward hatches. (Imperial War Museum)

94. The Medjerda valley provided a gap in the enemy's mountain defences through which two British armoured divisions, the 6th and

7th, could be unleashed on to the plain beyond, so bringing the war in Africa to an end. No fewer than five Churchill regiments – the North Irish Horse, 12 and 48 RTR, and 142 and 145 Regiments RAC – supported the infantry in bitter fighting for the high ground which dominated the valley, but on 6 May the last objective was taken. (Imperial War Museum)

95. A British field battery receives an enthusiastic welcome from the citizens of Tunis. The vehicle nearest the camera was known as a Quad, or more officially as the Morris Four-Wheel-Drive Artillery Tractor, and was the standard towing vehicle for the legendary 25pdr gun-howitzer and its limber, for which it also accommodating the gun crew. The Quad had the appearance of being lightly armoured, but it was not: for a while, Rommel used a captured example as a mobile command post. (USAMHI)

95▶

▼94

▲96 ▼97

96. The first troops to enter Tunis were armoured car patrols from, respectively, 'C' Squadron 1st Derbyshire Yeomanry and 'B' Squadron 11th Hussars, which reached the centre of the city at 15.40hrs. on 7 May 1943. The Eleventh's distinctive badgeless brown beret with its cherry-coloured band was universally known throughout the desert and recognized even by the Afrika Korps. In June 1940, armed with ancient Rolls-Royce and Morris armoured cars, the Cherrypickers, as they were known, had fired the first shots in the Desert War; now, equipped with Daimlers, it was fitting that they should witness the last, almost three years later. (Imperial War Museum)

97. Philosophic Germans surrender in droves outside the gates of Tunis. The Sherman belongs to the 22nd Armoured Brigade (1

RTR, 5 RTR and 4th County of London Yeomanry), and the 7th Armoured Division's famous jerboa can be seen on the offside track guard, above the tactical number '67' which denotes the junior armoured regiment of the brigade. For the final offensive in Tunisia the 7th Armoured was transferred from the Eighth Army to the First. (Imperial War Museum)

98. This elderly White-Laffly armoured car, shown during the Allied victory parade in Tunis, saw widespread use in French colonial possessions prior to the Second World War. The vehicle mounted a 13.2mm cannon, had 14mm armour, weighed 7.5 tons, had a crew of four, and could, under extreme pressure, make 50mph. (USAMHI)

99. An American infantryman dives for cover as a Lee moves forward to suppress sniper fire. When it came to street fighting the Lee had a definite edge over the Sherman in that while its 75mm main armament engaged targets ahead the 37mm in the top turret could simultaneously fire at those on the flanks. Bizerta, 8 May 1943. (USAMHI)

100. Another view of the street fighting in Bizerta, 8 May 1943. The

tank crew have opened up, apparently satisfied that they have dealt with the sniper threat, although the vehicle commander continues to wear his steel helmet and the infantry (extreme right) are still moving warily. The troops are keeping a sensible distance behind the tank, thereby reducing the risk of casualties from ricochets off the armour. (USAMHI)

▼100

101. The American unit identification code is clearly visible on the bumper of this engineer halftrack, seen in Bizerta shortly after the fighting ceased. The code '9-15E-B-35' breaks down as follows: 9 = 9th Infantry Division; 15E = 15th Engineer Battalion; B = Company 'B'; 35 = 35th vehicle. (USAMHI)

102. In North Africa the Churchill's 6pdr did not fire an HE shell, which placed the tank at a serious disadvantage when dealing with anti-tank guns. A further hindrance was that the recessed mantlet was not proof against bullet splash around the interior edges. An ingenious solution to both problems was provided by Capt. Percy Morrell of the Royal Electrical and Mechanical Engineers, who successfully fitted the Churchill turret with a 75mm Sherman gun and mantlet. Altogether some 200 of these conversions were made at 665 Tank Troop's workshops at Le Khroub, Algeria, and subsequently saw service in Italy, the vehicle being known as the NA 75 (North African, 75mm). The photograph shows the prototype conversion. (Maj. Percy Morrell)

▲103

103. The Sherman mantlet had a flat peripheral flange which was bolted directly on to the turret face, and to accommodate this a large hole was marked out on the face of the Churchill turret and then cut out. The front face of the Sherman turret was flat, but that of the Churchill was curved in the vertical plane so that it was necessary to rebate the cheeks on either side of the hole before offering the gun and mantlet. When a satisfactory seat had been obtained, the mantlet was arc-welded to the turret. (Author)

104. Among the many technical problems encountered by Morrell was the fact that in the Churchill the loader was located on the right of the gun with the breech opening towards him, whilst in the

Sherman this position was reversed. The difficulty was solved by turning the gun through 180 degrees, which meant that the traverse controls had to be re-located and the elevating gear fitted with a cross-over linkage. The butt of the co-axial Browning was then found to ground on the power traverse equipment, so the mounting was modified to follow the main armament up to the point where the butt grounded (left) and then remain static while the 75mm continued upwards, the small degree of use so lost being considered acceptable. The re-positioning of the main armament meant that the breech-mechanism lever (BML) was now on top of the gun. (Maj. Percy Morrell)

▼104